A SCRUFFY HUSBAND IS A HAPPY HUSBAND

...And other real stories from the lighter side of marriage

50

A SCRUFFY HUSBAND IS A HAPPY HUSBAND
...And other real stories from the lighter side of marriage

Edited and authenticated by
Ron R. Lee

PUBLISHING
Pomona, California

A SCRUFFY HUSBAND IS A HAPPY HUSBAND
Copyright © 1991 by Christianity Today Incorporated

Library of Congress Cataloging-in-Publication Data

Lee, Ron R.
  Scruffy husbands : real stories from the lighter side / narrated and authenticated by Ron R. Lee.
    p.   cm.
  Includes index.
  ISBN 1-56179-025-7 : $6.99
  [1. Husbands—Humor. 2. Marriage—Humor.] I. Title.
PN6231.H8L4   1991
818'.5407—dc20   91-17138
                                                                        CIP

Published by Focus on the Family Publishing, Pomona, CA 91799
Distributed in the U.S.A and Canada by Word Books, Dallas, Texas

Editors: Keith Wall and Janet Kobobel
Cover and interior illustrations: Steve Bjorkman
Book designer: Timothy Jones
Printed in the United States of America

91 92 93 94 95 96 / 10 9 8 7 6 5 4 3 2 1

*This book is dedicated
to the women who married
us and help us find the
humor in everyday marriage.*

Contents

Acknowledgments

Many people had a part in the production of this book, some of whom I work closely with, and others whom I haven't even met. Thanks go to Harold Myra, who first came up with the idea of putting together a book that would allow men to take a look at the lighter side of marriage. Thanks also to the writers who were willing to tell real stories from their own marriages for the benefit of you, the reader. And finally, my gratitude goes to the editorial staff of *Marriage Partnership* magazine—Harold Smith, Elizabeth Newenhuyse, Marian Liautaud and Gregg Lewis—for helping to generate ideas for this book and then evaluating these stories as they came in.

Ron R. Lee

Chapter One

GET REAL!
Mixing It Up With
the Perfect Husband

By R.U. Shure

This book contains stories from a variety of husbands, each of whom will own up to any number of failings. They're honest about it, so I'm not revealing anything they wouldn't tell you themselves. But before we get to their stories, we thought we would show you an interview with a different kind of married man—the Perfect Husband. To obtain this exclusive report, we asked R.U. Shure, a frequent contributor to Marriage Partnership *magazine, to go a few rounds with this "legend" of a man. We were certain that Shure, a go-for-the-jugular journalist if I ever saw one, was the right guy for the job. Being a less-than-perfect husband himself, Shure was eager to draw a bead on this "model" husband. But I'll let him tell you the story. He was there when it happened.*

Ron R. Lee

I had read about the legendary Perfect Husband in a number of books and in *Ladies' Home Journal,* but I had never actually met him. So when the editors of *Marriage Partnership* asked me to interview him, I jumped at the chance.

I'm sure you've heard about this guy. He keeps his family cars running to perfection but also cooks four nights a week. He helps with laundry and vacuuming but never gets behind on home repairs. He holds his own in a fast-track career but never misses one of the kids' piano recitals.

I met him for lunch at a diner near his office. He ate a man-sized roast beef sandwich and a green salad. And he didn't put sugar or cream in his coffee. I pulled out my reporter's notebook and turned on the tape recorder. This day I would take no prisoners. There was just no way he could be as great as everyone had made him out to be.

I can believe that you keep on top of your yard work, but how are you at auto repair, really?

Actually, I'm incredibly adept at it. Once, I was driving on the Kansas Turnpike when my muffler dropped down and started scraping against the pavement. I set the cruise control on sixty-five, opened the car door, leaned down and tied the muffler up with a wire coat hanger. It didn't cost a cent, and I still made it to the next rest stop before Billy's bladder exploded.

I notice you're eating a roast beef sandwich. Don't you think it's better to avoid red meat?

Not in my case. I take care of my health by working out seven times a week. But I'm not overly vain. I just look good automatically. For example, I get a haircut every three weeks—but I never look like I just got a haircut.

Doesn't your vigorous workout schedule take time away from your kids?

Not at all. I spend several hours every night helping them with their homework, and I coach my son's Little League team. But I never harangue the players. I just tell them to have fun and not to worry about winning. But they do win. In fact, my team goes undefeated every season.

I've heard your wife doesn't enjoy sports. How do you square your heavy involvement in Little League baseball with your wife's need to share interests as a couple?

It's no problem, really. I love to entertain. I'm always initiating social engagements. And when we have friends over, I never fail to clean up afterward. But at the same time I don't have a desperate need to have people around. I'm a rugged individualist; I need my space. I go out and climb a mountain every once in a while. But it doesn't take any time away from my family.

A lot of men have trouble talking to their sons about sex. Have you found that to be a problem?

Never. I'm perfectly comfortable talking about sex, and I'm remarkably well informed. I have all the correct information and nomenclature, even about women.

I've heard that you always leave work on time, but surely you've been delayed getting home at least once by a traffic jam or a flat tire. C'mon, be honest. Haven't you ever been late for dinner?

Just once, and I made sure to call my wife from a pay phone so she wouldn't worry. Of course, I was late only because I was helping a guy out. His car was sitting on the shoulder, and I stopped to overhaul his engine for him. It was a rare Italian sports car, and I was the only person within a 500-mile radius who knew how to repair it.

How does a model husband such as yourself deal with his in-laws?

First, I never complain about going to visit them. In fact, when we plan vacations, I usually suggest taking my wife's parents with us. Just last summer we all went to the Grand Canyon in a nine-by-twelve-foot pop-up camper.

I've read that you're unfailingly polite and considerate of others' feelings. How have you been able to remain a true gentleman without offending feminists?

Well, I always help my wife with her coat, and I open doors even for strangers. But I'm an extra-perceptive guy. I'm always sensitive to women who don't want that sort of attention.

You seem to lead an incredibly busy—yet perfectly balanced—life. Are you able to free up any time for hobbies?

The truth is, I'm kind of a Renaissance man. After I've put the kids to bed and I'm finished with the dishes, I relax by playing the piano. In fact, I could have been a concert pianist had I not gone into brain surgery. But that ended up taking too much time away from my family, so I decided to work with the underprivileged. It's a not-for-profit organization, but it pays super well.

Any closing thoughts?

Just that I'm totally at peace with who I am. I'm not threatened by my fast-track colleagues. I never compare myself with others, but I'm not complacent either. I'm always ready to move up the corporate ladder. But even when I do become CEO of a Fortune 500 corporation, it won't take any time away from my family.

That, it seems, is how the Perfect Husband is presented to a gullible American public. But, being a seasoned reporter and a married man himself, R.U. Shure didn't believe a word of it. And neither do we. The popular image of manly perfection, after all, is a myth.

That's why, in the following eighteen chapters, we deal with marriage in the rough-and-tumble world real husbands face in the 1990s. We're talking about exposés on why toilets get clogged when you're trying to leave for work; the mystery of empty gas tanks; the benefit of worn-out clothes; why wives like to plant things; the adventure of budget motels; the challenges of buying a Christmas tree; do-it-yourself home security; and, of course, the ever-popular topic in locker rooms everywhere: the women in our lives, especially the ones we're married to.

This book looks at marriage as it really is, through the eyes of hard-working, big-hearted, well-meaning husbands. None of these men is a flawless model—for which we can be thankful. But each acknowledges that marriage, even when it's aggravating, can sometimes be quite funny. And for that we are grateful indeed.

Chapter Two

CLOGGED PLUMBING
My Adventure
With a Plumber's Snake

By Kevin A. Miller

*Kevin Miller is a writer, an editor, a husband and a
father. He's also a very funny man. That, in part, is
why he wrote three of the chapters in this book. But
ask Kevin about the funniest person he's ever known,
and he'll tell you about his old college roommate.
"This guy swam in the college fountain, did the polka
late at night in the street, tied me into bed while I was
sleeping and set up a rubber dart gun so it would
shoot me when I opened the closet door." A regular
barrel of laughs, to be sure. But none of those antics
hold a candle to the time Kevin tried to fix the toilet in
his suburban Chicago home.*

The other night I flipped on the light switch in the bathroom.
The light over the medicine chest flickered and then went
dark.

I may not know much about electricity, I thought, *but I am a
husband, and husbands are supposed to fix things.* I figured this
to be an easy, five-minute job. Call a professional? No way.

I flipped off the circuit breaker and took out the switchbox. It
was connected to only a few wires: a red, a black, an orange and

7

two whites. In a few seconds I had the wire positions memorized. But when I came home from the store with the new switchbox, I noticed it was different from the old one.

No big deal, I thought. But with a couple more screws on the left side, I began to get confused about how the old piece had been wired. *Let's see, it was an orange, a white and a black on the left, a red and a white on the right. Or was it an orange on the right? No, because the white was on top of the black.*

I screwed on the wires as best I could remember. Back in the garage I pushed over the circuit breaker, which was immediately destroyed by an enormous blue spark. Meanwhile, the bathroom was still dark, and I was standing in a cold, black garage, wondering what to do next.

In a strange way, I realized, this fiasco actually began on my wedding day nearly ten years ago. That's when, before God and a large company of witnesses, I vowed to love, cherish and protect my wife. The day after the wedding, however, I learned that unwittingly I had also agreed to fix, clean and maintain our car, apartment and sundry possessions. This is the universally accepted Husband's Role. And sometimes I suspect my wife, Karen, regrets it.

Some people are hearing-impaired; I am repair-impaired. For me, "home improvement" is a contradiction in terms.

Above some of the pictures hanging in our home are three holes from aborted attempts to place the nails accurately. My living room carpet has almost recovered from the time I spilled water trying to empty our old hot water heater. And two of our closet doors still bear scars from The Battle of the Closet Door Hanging. By the time I finish a project, our property value has declined.

But fixing things is my job. That's what a husband is for. So when repairs are called for, I rush into action. Fortunately for my sake, I'm not left *completely* to my own devices. There is a

Bumbling Handyman's Code, passed on since the dawn of time, when cavehusbands first tried to caulk drafty caves to impress their cavewives. The Code includes these unalterable laws:

1. The job will come at the worst possible time, such as when it is dark and rainy; an hour *after* you were supposed to have the moving van loaded; or in the middle of the seventh game of the World Series.

2. You will never have done this particular job before. Nor will your fix-it manuals offer any information about it.

3. The warranty will have expired the month before. And even if it's still in effect, it won't matter because:
   a. you lost the warranty in your last move; or
   b. you failed to fill out the warranty registration card and mail it back to the manufacturer.

4. Local building codes are never as tough as your wife's. A woman is gifted with the ability to detect a crooked picture on a living room wall while driving by someone's house. Among the other areas wives will notice (and not bend on) are:
   a. The placement of a chair rail. (You will always put it too high.)
   b. The tint of interior paint. (Your paint store may use a sophisticated, computerized color-analysis matching system. It doesn't matter. The paint will still be "a little too peach, don't you think?" in relation to the carpet.)

5. The store with the part you need closes in ten minutes. And you live twelve minutes away.

6. You won't have the right tool. You will then have the brilliant idea that you don't need the right tool because, after all, you have this other tool that ought to do much the same thing.

Resist this urge.

I learned the hard truth about using the wrong tool one morning when our toilet clogged. I was dressed in suit and tie and about to leave for work. But it being our only bathroom, I couldn't leave Karen stranded for the day. *No need to change clothes,* I figured. *Just grab the plunger, give a few up-and-downs, and the pipe will flow as freely as Niagara Falls.*

I looked for the plunger. *Drat. I left it in the basement. Forget running down two flights of stairs and back up. Why, right over here there's a toilet brush that ought to work fine.* I picked up the brush—an oval ring covered with white plastic bristles—and *en garde!* I plunged it into the bowl.

Thrust one, parry two, and . . . unnh. Stuck. I pulled. I pulled again, harder. Still I couldn't pull it out. Somehow I had gotten the brush head lodged in the drain hole of the toilet bowl, and the brush wasn't budging.

This is silly, I thought. *Of course it's got to come out.* I bent down, grabbed the handle with both hands, gave a herculean pull and . . . snap. I went flying backward through the shower curtain and into the bathtub.

I looked up at my hand, which was firmly gripping the *handle* of the toilet brush. The head was still in the toilet. Oh boy. I climbed out of the tub, glanced fearfully at the toilet, and then ran down two flights of stairs, grabbed the plunger and puffed back upstairs.

"Maybe the suction of the plunger will move this baby," I said to myself. Thirty plunges later the water had receded a few inches, but the so-called weightier matters hadn't budged because the toilet brush head was in the way. This plumbing war was escalating; now I was twenty minutes late for work.

I took off my suit coat and called my friend Paul, now at work, and begged him to come rescue me. He showed up twenty minutes later with a plumber's snake, a flexible metal rod that looks like an instrument of torture. The plan was to thread the snake past the brush head and pull it back; the brush head would pop out like toast from a toaster. Or so the plan went. Fifteen minutes later, all we'd managed to do was make the plumber's snake awfully stinky.

My friend and I figured it was time for all-out war. We shut off the water. We disconnected the pipes going into the toilet. Then we unbolted the toilet from the floor. With a grunt, we lifted the toilet and leaned it over the edge of the bathtub while the contents oozed out. Then we set it back on the floor and stared at it.

No good husband would stand to be defeated by a repair project. I reached slip-joint pliers down into the bowl, and a few pulls later I had my toilet brush head, the one with the brown plastic bristles.

It only took us another forty-five minutes to get the toilet bolted back down and the pipes hooked up. So what if I was two hours late for work? By doing it myself, I had gained that inestimable feeling that every husband feels when he tackles a project—and really mucks it up.

But hey, who cares if I don't know a socket wrench from Silly Putty? Karen loves me anyway (though I'm careful not to ask her in the midst of a home-repair project).

Chapter Three

THE HOPELESS ROMANTIC

A Cold Kiss

By Nate Adams

*Nate Adams has family ties that run long and deep.
He remembers occasions when the extended family
would gather and exchange sentimental memories in
long, nostalgic conversations. Here's how Nate
describes it (with a little embellishment): "An aunt
would turn to an uncle and, with a frighteningly sentimental look in her eyes, ooze, 'Oh, honey, tell about
the night you proposed to me.' The uncle would
mutter something like, 'Awwww,' before trying to
bounce the question back to her under the guise that
she could tell it much better than he. If that didn't
work, he would simply dump his iced tea in his lap,
excuse himself and leave the room." That sort of
thing helps explain why Nate wanted his proposal of
marriage to be an unforgettable event.*

Beth and I had been dating for more than six years, and most
of our friends had pretty much given up on our ever getting
married. So when I finally decided the time was right to ask Beth
to marry me, I knew the proposal had to be special.

Our friends would want to know every detail, if only to confirm that an official engagement had actually occurred. Besides, I had the opportunity to create a memory that would be retold in our family for years to come. This event couldn't be ordinary. And it wouldn't be easy, either.

In our case, the ring couldn't be part of the surprise. Most guys can outdo themselves when it comes to creative ways of presenting an engagement ring, like baking it in lasagna and then performing a quick Heimlich maneuver.

But I didn't have that advantage since I couldn't predict what kind of ring Beth would like. Many times I had slyly sidetracked a shopping mall date to the jewelry store window and pointed out the rings I thought she'd like. This always guaranteed a good laugh.

A surprise ring was out, so some other romantic symbol would have to do. I scoured my brain before it came to me—a long-stemmed rose. She could press it between the pages of a large book and uncover it years later, no doubt prompting a starry-eyed kiss on my seventy-year-old cheek.

That settled it. I'd give her a rose, and I'd propose to her at the site of our first kiss! Now, the timing. Christmas was coming up, but that would be too predictable. Before or after the holiday would be better. Then I remembered my parents were married two days before Christmas. I could propose on the eve of their wedding, tying in to family heritage and tradition, which are always high on the romance scale.

The rose, the place, the date. All that remained was implementation. That's when the best-laid plans of this hopeless romantic began to deteriorate. As I headed out the door with rose in hand, I began to wonder: *How do you conceal a long-stemmed rose?* There wasn't enough time to plant it at the site of the proposal. I was already running late for our date. (We were supposedly going shopping at a mall near the college campus where we first kissed.)

I hurriedly laid the rose between my driver's seat and the car door. It was out of Beth's sight, and as long as I kept the window cracked the fragrance wouldn't be noticeable. I'd figure out a concealment plan for the surprise presentation during our twenty-minute car ride. Probably.

I picked up Beth, and as we drove to our romantic destiny, the freezing rain that had been pelting our windshield turned to sleet. We bantered lightly, talking mainly about why I had my window down during a sleet storm. Eventually the conversation turned to windshield defogging principles that I was relating as quickly as I could make them up.

Then we pulled into the college campus and Beth's suspicion kicked in. "What are you doing?" she asked.

"Oh, I thought it would be a nice evening for a walk," I replied. Unfortunately, my prerehearsed response didn't take into consideration the current sleet storm.

Maybe she just trusted me. Or maybe she was hoping that I meant a walk inside the gymnasium. But Beth played along with my clumsy lead in a way she has since mastered thanks to five years of practice.

"Oh. That sounds . . . lovely!" she said, pulling her jacket collar up and looking at her feet for boots that weren't there.

Did I mention that the site of our first kiss was in left field of the college's baseball field? Of course, the original kiss was on a balmy evening in early September, not during a sleet storm in late December.

I parked the car near the ball field, feeling like a bank robber whose master plan had been foiled. I turned to my hostage and said, "Well, shall we?"

As Beth stepped out her side of the car into a puddle, I pulled off a rose-concealment solution that could only have been inspired by twenty minutes of sleet blowing hard against the side of my head. I inserted the petals of the rose up under the waistline of my jacket, sliding the stem up along my rib cage until I felt the near-frozen petals on my neck. Propping the bottom of the stem in my pants pocket, I buttoned the top button of my jacket collar and set off walking with a ramrod-straight posture that would have made my eighth-grade piano teacher proud.

Beth was still playing along admirably, but with each squish of her foot the questions grew more skeptical. "Will this be a *long* walk?" she asked. "Where *exactly* are we going?"

There were other questions, but I've forgotten the ones that didn't contribute to the romance of the moment. Besides, I was a man on a mission, and if Romeo could die for Juliet, surely I could make it across the third base line through conditions conquerable by any garden-variety mail carrier.

At last we were there. Left field.

"I suppose you're wondering why I've brought you out here on a night like this," I began.

"Well, yes . . . ," she replied sweetly, though her eyes were saying, "You've got less than sixty seconds to bring this whole thing to a point before you slide into home plate headfirst."

Then I did it. In a personal, intimate moment, I asked her to marry me. And she said yes.

She threw her arms around me in a tight bear hug. I'll never forget the tingling sensation I felt up and down my rib cage. The rose I had carried like a man with a back ailment was now drawing blood. I quickly removed the thorny surprise and presented it to Beth, clarifying my explanation of why I had jumped out of her embrace with a scream of pain.

We walked back to the car and proceeded to the college's Fine Arts building to find a piano. I sat down at the keyboard and played the song I'd written for Beth shortly after we met, adding a verse that commemorated this newest chapter of our life together.

That my wife can look back on my marriage proposal and see magical romance is still amazing to me. But I'm committed to keep on trying. You should hear what I have planned for our next anniversary!

Chapter Four

CAR AND DRIVER
My Van, and
Why I Bought It

By William H. Willimon

*College football does funny things to people. Take
Will Willimon, for example. He's a well-educated,
widely read man with a responsible, high-profile job.
(He's dean of the chapel at Duke University.) But
that's not all. He's also a football fanatic when it
comes to the Duke University Blue Devils. That's why
he got out of bed one morning and bought a conversion van. Or at least that's the way he explains it.*

O ne Saturday morning in the fall of 1987, I found myself
browsing through the newspaper, looking at ads for conversion vans. They were expensive, so I decided to forget about
whatever I was thinking when I initially turned to the automo-
tive section.

"I know what you're looking for," said my wife, Patsy. "I saw
it on a used-car lot last week. A completely tasteless blue van."

This woman who chose to marry someone like *me* is now lec-
turing me on good taste? But she did say "blue," as in Duke
University *Blue* Devils, so ten minutes later we were on the lot
looking at a Dodge van. It was two years old and had blue shag
carpeting, curtains with blue velour tiebacks and running

19

boards.

"Mr. Williston," said the salesman, "unlike a lot of these conversion vans, this one is done in good taste. You don't see curtains with blue velour tiebacks in many of them. And nothing brings a family together like a van."

"How many miles does it get per gallon of gas?" I asked.

"Mr. Williamson," he answered, "as they say, 'If you got to ask, you can't afford it.'"

For some reason, all of this made perfect sense to me, and we bought the van. The next morning Patsy and I arose early and peered into our garage. "We really did buy a van," I said. "What was I doing? Was I drunk?"

"Of course not," said Patsy. "You're a Methodist."

"Well," I announced, "I'm going to drive that van when Duke is invited to a bowl game." (I said this even though the only person I had ever met who had seen Duke play in a bowl had grandchildren.)

"You really are crazy," my wife said. "First you buy a van with curtains and velour tiebacks, then you talk about going with Duke to a bowl game. Any time you want to come back to planet earth, just let me know."

The van took over our entire garage. We had to move out the lawnmower, the dog and everything else to make room for it. And it was so tall, we had to prop up the garage door with a rake just to get the thing inside.

But that's not all. The following Sunday a professor at the medical school was coming out of the University Chapel, where I hold forth every week, and said, "Some student parked this unbelievable blue van in your parking place, Will."

"That's *my* van," I said defensively.

"Your van!" he exclaimed. "That can't be. It has white stripes down the side, running boards, blue velour tiebacks."

"At least it's all done in good taste," I said.

"It is not," he retorted. "It looks ridiculous."

Then I ran into Charles Putman, Duke's provost. "Where did you get the money to buy that thing?" he asked. Charles is from Texas, so I knew he was green with envy over the curtains with the blue velour tiebacks.

"I'll be driving it to the bowl game, whenever Duke gets invited," I said. "If you promise to act right, you can go with me."

During the months that followed I guess I got a little loose and invited a number of other people to ride in my van if Duke ever went to a bowl. It had become a joke around our house, the kind of thing you sometimes say like, "When I get a million dollars . . ." or "When they elect me king. . ." My wife thought that, given time and patience, it was something I would get over. Like the measles.

Then came the fall of 1989 and Duke's victories over Northwestern, Maryland and Clemson. Winning was great, but it dawned on me that I had a problem. There was talk of a bowl game, and people started telling me I had invited them to ride in my van, including people I didn't even know. Of course, I never had any idea I would actually have to make good on those offers.

I should have been more sensible. But then again, if I had been that sort of person I wouldn't have bought a conversion van in the first place. So I decided to let those people fend for themselves, and Patsy and I went to the bowl game alone.

As we drove, I realized I had played an important role in Duke's trip to Birmingham and the American Bowl. That trip began one Saturday, two years earlier, when I awoke and felt the urge to buy a van. With that, I became the first person to make a concrete, visible commitment to winning football, and I never wavered.

"These are the virtues that made this country great," I say.

"That is the sort of reasoning that leads to the federal budget deficit, acid rain and war," says Patsy.

My wife is a wonderful person, but she hates to admit when she's wrong.

Chapter Five

OLD CLOTHES
A Scruffy Man
Is a Happy Man

By Harold Myra

*In times past Harold Myra served in a campus
ministry, and Jeanette Austin was a student involved
in the organization's activities. Harold says the things
he admired about Jeanette back then are the same
things he values today, namely "her vivacity and our
mutual commitments." The Myras eventually got
married, added five children to their family, and
recently celebrated their twenty-fifth wedding anniversary. But one thing about Harold still mystifies
Jeanette: His love of old clothes.*

I'm convinced most men love clothes that are, to put it mildly,
well-worn. The first man who demonstrated this magnificent truth to me was my neighbor when I was a teenager.

The man was wealthy. This we knew because he drove a new
car, worked on Wall Street and had a summer home next door to
our year-round one in the mountains.

He was also ambitious. He mowed, raked, painted, laid concrete and generally manicured his house, grounds and the
beachfront property across the road. His surroundings were
organized, spruced up, classy.

25

Precisely the opposite of his personal appearance.

His hat was bent over like crumpled cardboard. His saggy pants were ripped; his flannel shirt and jacket looked like rejects from some ancient hunting trip. His shoes were torn and cracked. And all colors of paint—faded and new—decorated his hat, shirt, pants and shoes. He let his beard grow, too, so that by Sunday afternoon, he looked totally scruffy—and happy.

All of this seemed to me, as a teenager, a wonderful freedom—a rich man looking like a bum.

His wife also worked outside a lot, but she looked properly sporty. Almost elegant. And I often wondered how she liked staring at her scruffy husband over lunch.

Which brings to mind my own wife's trials. Jeanette suffers like many women, wondering why her husband shows so little interest in new clothes. Why is it that so many men love the feel and familiarity of old clothes—and hate the prospect of shopping for their more fashionable replacements?

I admit there are women who love old skirts and blouses, and men who enjoy shopping for new clothes. But not many. Ever notice the large percentage of mall space devoted to women's clothing and accessories? I figure that in an average mall, women's clothing shops outnumber men's at least ten to one.

While women love to shop for new clothes, men would generally rather go to jail for a day than try on a new suit. Every once in a while, Jeanette will try to lure me to a special sale for men. But it's like dragging our dog over to converse with the cat. Eventually, we end up in the women's department instead, which is actually not a whole lot better since it still involves those boring racks and racks of clothes.

When I do have to stay in the men's section, I have a strategy: Get it over with and don't come back. I've been known to buy three suits in an hour—enough to last me for years to come.

And it's not just suits. Some time ago I went to a blue-jeans sale and bought three pair. Now, they are frayed and torn. The pockets are worn through. Even my teenage kids tell me those jeans are *not* cool.

So why do I love these old jeans? Simple. Every rip in the knees holds a memory, every frayed fiber a history of moments in the den or with friends and family.

I'm that way about a lot of the faded shirts and pants in my closet—even the ancient polyesters, once considered the latest and best when my generation was considered the latest and best. Think of the indignity of throwing these keepsakes into the garbage! Would you toss your wedding photos into the Goodwill box?

Admittedly, not every man is like me. Some, judging by their appearance, love to buy and wear the latest fashions and unceremoniously toss out everything that has become outdated. But I have a theory about this. These men, so awesomely attired, are actually closet old-clothes buffs. Deep within, they would love to let go and look just like my old neighbor in his saggy pants.

The seed for this theory was planted when I was fresh out of college and helping a concert touring group. Before the performance, I ended up dressing in the same room with the star of the show. This man was the ultimate. His clothes exuded the proper ambiance, the perfect cut.

The star was standing near me, holding his pants and about to put them on, when I noticed something astounding. He had raggedy underwear. I don't mean slightly frayed. I mean threadbare and ripped!

It was a revelation. I had watched this man perform in his flawless wardrobe. And now this! His true self standing in those shorts.

You may reject my theory out of hand, but think about it. All those stylish men—never admitting it to themselves—feeling subconsciously the desire to let loose and love old, unstylish, snagged trousers. It made me feel a little more normal.

Recently my family practically forced me to buy a new outfit. I hate to admit it, but I actually enjoyed looking up-to-date and unfaded. I even went so far as to toss out some *very* old shirts and slacks.

Yet as I threw them away, I felt a pang of regret. If I had only painted a wall or two in them while wearing my old fishing hat, then given them just a few more years to age! Then I might have kept them forever, looking as outrageously comfortable— and happy—as my old neighbor in the mountains.

Chapter Six

WEEKENDS
My Dream of
a Perfect Saturday

By Kevin A. Miller

You might remember Kevin Miller as the guy who, while wearing a suit and tie, waged war against his toilet back in chapter 2. Well, he's back. This time he relates a tale about Saturdays and why his idea of a good time seldom jibes with his wife's.

66 **H** oney, you've got to get moving," Karen pleaded one Saturday morning about ten o'clock.

I shuffled slowly, in my bathrobe, to the kitchen. "Don't rush me," I said. "Good things take time—fine wine, aged cheese, me..."

"But we've got to get the lawn mowed before lunch," Karen broke in, "because after that the kids go down for naps, and the mower would wake them up."

"Look," I said, "with work Monday through Friday and church on Sunday, this is my one day to take it easy."

"I know," Karen replied, "but we've got a dozen things to do before the Coffmans come for dinner."

"It wasn't my idea to invite them," I protested.

"But you said it was okay. We need to get the grill ready and the dessert made. Besides, I've been chasing two kids all week. I was hoping you'd take over with them some today."

"Now wait," I said, folding my arms and leaning against the kitchen counter. "Have you ever tried to do house projects with two little kids supervising you? Last Saturday I was trying to replace the ballcock on the toilet, and I turned around just for a second. The next thing I knew, water was spraying all over the bathroom."

"Well, join the club!" she said. "How do you think I get anything done all week?"

If you're anything like us, you and your wife never envision the weekend's activities in quite the same way. For example, Karen's dream of the perfect Saturday goes like this: sleep in; have husband (already shaved and dressed) serve her breakfast in bed; have husband get the kids dressed and fed; get things done without children undoing much of it; and watch husband make phenomenal progress on the 368 broken, leaking and peeling items in and around the house.

Contrast this with *my* dream of a perfect Saturday: sleep in; eat breakfast (preferably served to me); read a magazine without interruptions; watch some sporting events on TV; take a nap; and, if all goes according to plan, romance my wife.

We long ago recognized this difference between us, so we started sitting down on Fridays and discussing our *expectations* for the following day. (Yes, we actually use the E-word.) To no one's surprise, our lists never match. At a recent family meeting, Karen's included: make dessert for Sunday's company, move the patio furniture into the shed, write the family newsletter, shop, spend time with the kids and stuff the visitors' brochures for church. The activities were noble, energetic, needed, productive. It was obvious they wouldn't do.

I counteroffered, "Sleep in and live the life of a Roman emperor (all grapes peeled, please)." I figure that if God had wanted us to do chores or chase kids on Saturday, he wouldn't have put so many great sports events on TV. I'm flexible, though. If work has to be done, I'll do it—provided I don't have to get cold, wet or messy, and I can do it during commercials. Something like, say, replacing a lightbulb.

I gained some insight into this phenomenon a few weeks ago while reading brochures in my doctor's waiting room. According to one pamphlet, most men are alike in this respect: After a major event, we experience a physical letdown—a withdrawal from the extra adrenalin we've been pumping. On Saturday, for example, we go cold turkey in adrenalin withdrawal. From Monday through Friday we've been getting up at six, going to meetings, rushing to meet deadlines. On Saturday our eyelids refuse to be disturbed before ten-thirty. In my case, I feel about as pleasant and tenderhearted as Bart Simpson in a bad mood.

Karen, on the other hand, saves her adrenalin burst for Saturday, when she knows I'll be there to help with the kids and she can Really Get Things Done. She starts laying out the day's chores and projects a couple of days in advance. The only thing I lay out ahead of time is the *TV Guide* and the remote control. So by Saturday at 10:00 A.M., she's going sixty-five miles an hour. I'm in the garage for repairs.

At this point I can almost hear you asking, "Is there any hope for couples afflicted by The Saturday Syndrome?" The answer, of course, is no. But through a process of bile and terror, I've learned a few ways to keep weekend grumpiness to a minimum.

The first key, men, is not to promise anything. Promises have a way of setting your wife's expectations in cement. So when Karen asks me, "Will you have time to fix the swing set?" I offer only, "It's on my list." I don't mention that it's project 369.

Second, I never give an estimated completion time for a weekend chore. The "easy, ten-minute job" is a myth fostered by hardware store commercials. Trust me: The people who produce those ads live in high-priced condos and hire people to do their repairs. They don't have kids clinging to their knees when they scrape paint, and they have never made three trips back to a store because they kept forgetting, losing or breaking something.

And most important, look for excuses to get—and to give—some pampering. I've overheard more than one wife say, "Men are such babies when they get tired." Hey, if the diaper fits, wear it. I don't mind admitting that on some weekends I can use some pampering. And so can Karen.

I also keep my eyes open to opportunities for romance. If something has to be cut from Saturday's list, it won't be a date with my wife. That means that come next spring, we'll still have leaves in our yard from the previous fall. But at least we're not as grumpy about it.

Chapter Seven

A PERSONAL GAS CRISIS
The Chrysler
That Ran on Air

By Ron R. Lee

*In some ways, I'm not your typical guy. Back in
high school, for example, I drove a forty-year-old
Ford and loved it. Now, more than two decades later,
I still reserve a special place in my heart for old cars.
My wife hasn't always understood this die-hard loy-
alty to geriatric modes of transportation, especially
one summer when we were relying on an aging
Chrysler to get us safely to St. Louis.*

When I was a boy, my dad used to say I reminded him of a
mule. My mother called me hardheaded. And my sister,
when the occasion warranted, would just haul off and hit me.

They assumed I was just plain stubborn. But I'm not, really.
It's more that I make a decision—based on reason and logic—
and stick with it.

My rational bent worked all right until I got married. That's
when I discovered that my wife approaches life from the opposite direction. I can show Jeanette the latest research findings
from M.I.T., a computer spread sheet and a recommendation
from *Consumer Reports*—all in support of my conclusion—
but if it doesn't "feel" right to her, the decision is wrong. That's

just the way she is.

When we first got married, our different ways of approaching life would bump into each other every now and then. But we were always able to reach a satisfactory compromise. That is until Jeanette's feelings got into a shoving match with my logic one hot July afternoon when we were traveling west on Interstate 270 in downstate Illinois. Here's how it happened.

We had invited three nephews and a niece to spend a week with us in the Chicago suburbs. At the end of their visit we got ready to drive them home to St. Louis. I had gassed up our 1973 Chrysler the day before—a good thing, since the bicycle rack clamped to the rear bumper prevented easy access to the gas tank.

Off we drove, a sauna-like wind blowing through the open windows. Except for heavy road noise and the threat of windburn, the trip went fine. That is, until the LOW FUEL light blinked on.

"The fuel light is on," Jeanette alerted me.

"I see it," I responded.

"Aren't you going to stop for gas?"

"Yes."

But I didn't say when. I was pretty sure the light meant we had five gallons left. At fifteen miles per gallon, we could travel another seventy-five miles. And we were only sixty miles from the Texaco station where we usually refill the tank on these trips.

I kept driving while I considered the remote possibility that I had miscalculated. I was as sure as anyone could be that we wouldn't run out of gas, but the possibility that Jeanette might be right added to the adventure. I had hit upon a convenient way to turn a trek across five hours of uneventful Illinois prairie into *Indiana Jones and the Gas Tank of Doom.*

My wife's voice yanked me out of my reverie. "Ron, we have

four kids in this car, and I don't want to get stranded on the road somewhere. Stop at the next exit and get some gas!"

I sensed Jeanette's heart wasn't in this adventure.

"We're not going to be stranded," I tried to reassure her. "I checked the roadside mile marker back there, and I figure we'll make it to the Texaco station with at least a gallon to spare." She wasn't reassured.

Within fifteen miles of our destination we ran into road construction. Two lanes narrowed to one, and the pounding of jackhammers joined the drone of the hot wind. This unexpected turn of events merely heightened my sense of adventure. I pictured us wheeling into the Texaco station, road dust covering the car, with less than a gallon to spare. It would prove once again that a logical decision is a dependable decision.

We hadn't driven more than two miles farther when I felt the engine give way. I surreptitiously shifted the car into neutral to lengthen our coasting distance. But I didn't do it surreptitiously enough.

"Did we just run out of gas?" Jeanette demanded.

God, whose goodness is not limited by logic (*or* by stubbornness), was about to spare my marriage. A sign announced the Wood River exit, which was handy since I had decided it was time to stop for gas. As Illinois topography goes, we should have found an exit ramp as flat as Rocky Marciano's nose. But this one sloped enough for us to coast to the bottom and run a stop sign.

I took a right and rolled to an intersection, where we encountered a traffic light. With adventure still hanging heavy in the July air, I ran the stop light and took another right.

We were only a hundred feet from a much-needed petroleum product. You may have trouble believing this, but our Chrysler (which is the size of a small house) coasted into the filling station entrance and stopped at a pump labeled "Regular."

I got out to take the bicycles off the rear bumper, and the kids went inside to use the bathroom. I pumped a capacity 24.2 gallons, put the bikes back on the rack, paid for the gas, and we all got back in the car. I sensed fumes, but it wasn't because I had spilled some Regular on my foot. Jeanette was hot.

"You see," I began to explain, "I forgot to factor in the added wind resistance created by the bicycles. That resulted in us getting less than the customary fifteen miles per gallon, causing us to run out of gas sooner than anticipated."

My wife didn't want a logical explanation. Instead, she wanted me to recognize that her feelings about stopping for gas fifty miles earlier had been the better part of wisdom.

"You're just lucky we ran out of gas near an exit," she reminded me. "And you're lucky there was enough of a slope that we could coast; and you're lucky there was no traffic so you didn't have to stop before you got to the gas station. We could have been stranded on the highway! Don't you have any common sense?"

I analyzed her question and decided the rational course of action would be not to answer. But I *was* thinking about what we had just experienced.

It's a good thing we're in this big old Chrysler, I told myself. *A Ford Escort never would have coasted all the way from the highway to that gas pump.*

I didn't share that thought with Jeanette, however, since she might have confused my love of old cars with stubbornness. Wives are like that sometimes.

Chapter Eight

SURPRISES
Who's That in My Bed?

By Rodney Clapp

Rodney Clapp has known his wife since their grade-school years in the small town of Forgan, Oklahoma. They didn't start dating each other until high school, but Rodney admits that Sandy's legs had caught his attention back in junior high. The Clapps got married while they were students at Oklahoma State University, and today they live in Illinois with their daughter, Jesselyn.

I rose and showered early that day. Brushing my teeth and shaving, I heard pots clanging and assumed Sandy was in the kitchen. I returned to the bedroom, bent down to pick my shirt up off the floor and suddenly heard a seductive voice: "Hello, handsome."

There I crouched, unarmored in anything but my Fruit of the Looms, hand frozen in a grasp on a flannel shirt. Two thoughts streaked into my mind at once: 1) There cannot be anyone else in the bedroom; 2) so who is the woman under the blankets?

My body was in an awkward position—my knees still bent, my hand immobile—but the human mind is forever trying to save dignity. It quickly suggested that there must be an explanation (maybe I heard the landlady downstairs preparing breakfast). My mind advised my body to do nothing foolish, simply

43

to look and see who was in the bed. But the human body, since caveman times, has been more concerned with survival than dignity. So now, still crouched, still holding the shirt, my body involuntarily jumped straight up. A foot or so. My arm waved the shirt spastically, like a flag of surrender. And, even as my mind tried to stifle it, my body squeezed a whoop of momentary terror up from my chest and out my wide-open mouth.

Only then did my body turn my head to see who was in the bed. Sandy's eyes were visible just above the edge of the blanket. She was rocking the bed in laughter.

We have been scaring each other ever since we moved into this big, three-bedroom apartment. Even after the bedroom episode, I wandered once into the kitchen and blurted out a question before Sandy realized I was there. Hand on her chest, she staggered backward in a half circle. She was pregnant then, and it's a terrible thing to see a woman five months with child looking like a drunk trying to go uphill against the wind. Now we try to warn each other we are coming, whistling or stomping our feet or knocking on the wall before entering a room.

It's odd, when you think about it, that after living together for eleven years, your wife remains alien enough to surprise you. You figure you've seen all her tricks and quirks. You know at which foods she will stick out her tongue. You know by her walk, when you pick her up after work and watch her approach the car, if it's been a good or bad day. You know, before she's read the funny pages, which cartoon she will put on the refrigerator.

But then one day she surprises you. And you notice anew the exact spot where the hairline begins on her forehead and the unique character of her hands. You realize what you had forgotten for a while—that she's not an extension of yourself, not a supporting actress in a private drama you are writing and directing.

I remember a particularly severe argument about six years ago. It involved not only the two of us but Sandy's parents as well. As far as I could see, Sandy had taken her parents' side against me. For two weeks we stalked sullenly round one another. I went home from work dreading the moment when our conversation would inevitably drift into The Argument. Before long she would start crying, and I would flee for a long walk.

One evening I returned home from the walk. Both of us freshly wounded, we found it in ourselves to be tender. Sandy tried, harder than before, to explain her position. I tried, harder than before, to listen. And then it became clear: Sandy wasn't simply taking sides. She understood my desires, but she was also empathizing with the pain this decision would cause her parents. The depth and ingenuity of her empathy were a revelation to me—so surprising it had taken me two weeks to see them.

Sometimes I look at Sandy sleeping, unaware of me, vulnerable as a child, and remember that she lived a good part of her life before I ever entered it. The face of a sleeping woman, of *this* sleeping woman, is profound. With its soft lines, with its hidden eyes, with its closed lips, it says: "Eleven years are barely enough to get beneath the skin—let alone to the heart—of the mystery that is a woman."

This woman is my wife. But she is also a sweet stranger, beyond the knowing of a lifetime. She surprises me, and I am glad for that because it renews our marriage. Even when she forgets to knock.

Chapter Nine

LOSING THINGS
Why Do Women Always Win at Lost and Found?

By Gregg Lewis

*Anyone who knows Gregg Lewis will tell you he's
not the most organized human being. But how could
he be? He has a wife, five kids and a dog. He works
out of his home as a full-time free-lance writer. Plus,
he coaches baseball, basketball and soccer; and he's
not afraid to head up the occasional church fund
drive. So who can blame him when, from time to time,
something gets misplaced? Actually, misplacing
things isn't the problem. It's finding them.*

For the longest time, I figured it must be women's intuition.
I just couldn't come up with any other explanation.

Consider this: An able-bodied, fully sighted husband can
venture into a tiny walk-in closet, wander around in there for
hours and never find the article of clothing he's searching for.
But when he finally admits defeat and calls out, "Honey, do you
know where my high school football sweater is?" his wife can
walk in, glance right, pivot left, shove aside the blue suit he
wore to church last Sunday and reveal his old letter sweater,
hanging in bold red relief next to his favorite green sportcoat.

How do women do that? None of the marriage books I've

read give a guy a clue. Sixteen years of firsthand experience haven't solved the mystery either.

It happened again just yesterday.

Debi asked me to get a can of pineapple from the pantry. I looked high and low, twice, before saying, "I think we're out of pineapple."

"No," she insisted. "I'm sure I've seen at least one more can in there. Check the very back of the third shelf."

I began again to shift and scrutinize every can, canister and cereal box. "No pineapple!" I finally announced with certainty.

"I'm sure it's there," Debi said as she walked over to look for herself. I stood right behind her, looking over her shoulder, planning to enjoy the satisfaction (just once) of saying "See, what'd I tell you!" when she too failed in the search.

She reached in, shoved a bottle of syrup over next to the grits, pushed aside a dusty jar of Mexican salsa, and there at the back of the shelf sat a can of pineapple.

I muttered an embarrassed "Oh!"

Debi, to her credit, said not a word. But silently I asked myself once again, *How do women do that?*

It's not just Debi. My mom has humiliated my dad the same way for nearly fifty years. And at least once every time I go home for a visit, Mom does it to me.

How can a woman, who has to think twice to remember the points of the compass when she's standing in her own backyard, know exactly where I left my baseball glove after the final game last summer?

First, my mother. Then my wife. Now (I cringe to admit it) it's my five-year-old daughter, Lisette. The other week my sons and I combed the entire house looking for three-year-old Benjamin's shoes (which invariably disappear when we're rushing to get somewhere on time). Finally I enlisted Lisette, who'd been waiting for us out in the van.

She promptly marched down the hall and turned into the boys' room, where she excavated a mountain of stuffed animals to unearth two small blue tennis shoes.

How do women do that?

When I was a kid, I suspected it was a motherhood survival technique. But Debi did it even before she became a mother. And Lisette is only five.

Call me paranoid if you want, but lately I've taken to wondering if it's all a plot, if women don't roust their daughters out of bed in the middle of the night for surreptitious search-and-find training that will enable them to humiliate men for the rest of their lives. But I hated to believe anything that perfidious of the women I love.

And yet, something very telling occurred the other night. I noticed our dog had lost his collar chain.

"Debi, did you take Galahad's choker off?" I asked.

"No, I thought you did."

"Have you seen it?" I asked.

When she said she hadn't, I began my search. I checked by the back door where we keep his leash. I walked all over the house, wherever I thought the dog had been. Nothing.

The boys were all watching TV. So I asked, "Have you guys seen the dog's collar?"

"Nope."

"Unh-uh."

"Ask Lisette, maybe she knows."

I found my daughter outside, riding her bike on the driveway. "Sweetheart," I asked, "do you know where Galahad's choker chain is?"

"Yep. It's in the living room," she replied innocently.

"It's not in the living room!" I declared. "I've looked there."

She shrugged. "I saw it in the living room last."

"Then show me where you saw it," I ordered her.

She climbed off her bike, and I followed her through the house to the living room. She walked to one of her slippers that lay in the middle of the floor, picked it up, plunged her hand down into the toe, pulled out the missing choker and gave me her most charming smile. "Here it is, right here!"

My immediate reaction was to shake my head and think once more to myself, "How did she do that?" But I was so glad to find the lost choker that I didn't seriously ponder the question again.

Until I woke up this morning . . . and the truth hit me. Lisette knew right where to find that choker because she was the one who had hidden it there!

How do women always know just where to find anything we men are looking for? They're the ones who hide them! So when we get frustrated enough to give up or ask for help, our wives (or mothers or daughters) always know right where to "discover" them for us.

I realize that raises a couple of other questions: How do women always know what to hide? And how do they know ahead of time just when we're going to be looking for it?

I figure it must be women's intuition.

Chapter Ten

BARGAINS
What's Wrong With
Cheap Motels?

By Ron R. Lee

*Here I am once again, willing to admit I'm not
always Joe Perfect when it comes to being a husband.
Take, for example, my eagerness to save money
whenever possible. Okay, I'm a thrifty guy. It's
nothing to be ashamed of. And my wife, Jeanette, is
learning to live with it. She was even a little amused
last summer when I asked the proprietor of a New
Mexico army-navy store if she would give me a
volume discount if I bought more than one pair of
surplus blue jeans. I didn't get the discount, but it
never hurts to ask. At any rate, I'm glad my wife has
learned to see some humor in my occasional bouts of
frugality, because on a trip early in our marriage she
had a little trouble laughing at our unusual situation.
Here's what happened.*

Jeanette and I aren't made of money, so when we travel we
avoid costly airfare by driving our station wagon instead. It
takes longer, of course, but it's not the driving that bothers us;
it's stopping for the night that tends to result in a tussle.

When it comes to choosing a motel, we're like two people on

a shopping spree, except one of us is headed off to Saks Fifth Avenue while the other is getting in line for the big Blemished Floor Sample Sale at Larry's Discount City.

To put it bluntly, I'm a Larry's shopper. And Jeanette isn't.

Our dueling perspectives didn't matter all that much until we went on one particular road trip together. As darkness fell, we found ourselves in the clutches of two disagreements: when to stop and find a motel and how much to pay once we found one. Jeanette prefers getting off the interstate around 5:00 P.M. and finding a room at a Sheraton or Holiday Inn, or at the very least a Days Inn. Then she likes to unload the car, take a swim, eat a leisurely dinner and repair to the motel room to watch TV and relax.

I'm of a different school of thought. I figure that once you begin a road trip, the primary objective is to reach your destination. One shouldn't waste time lollygagging around at motels along the way. Instead, one should make the best use of one's time by driving until one can't keep his eyes open any longer. Then and only then do you get off the interstate—and pray you'll find a motel with a vacancy.

And, as a dedicated Larry's shopper, I figure a person should spend as little as possible on a motel room. That's why I steer clear of the national chains in favor of humble-looking local establishments. Something like Ed and Wanda's or the Dragem Inn. If it has a lock on the door, curtains on the windows, indoor plumbing and a bed, I'm happy.

As it turned out, my line of reasoning didn't impress Jeanette as we were pulling off the interstate late one night. The sign indicated we were exiting at a place called Alcatraz, or maybe it was Sing Sing. I don't remember exactly, but I do know it was a town with a prison's name. But I wasn't worried. We had once stayed in a motel named San Quentin, and it was by far the most luxurious cheap motel we had ever seen. I was hoping this experience would rival it.

I spotted a sign in the distance. It said Expressway Stay or something like that. When I pulled up in front of the office, Jeanette pointed out that there was a busy truck stop and a noisy beer joint next door. I told her not to worry, some locals were probably just stopping by to watch a ball game on their way home from work.

Luckily, the Expressway Stay had a vacancy *and* it was reasonably priced. (Just $21.97 for the two of us. My idea of road-trip heaven.) We drove the car down to Room 134, unloaded our luggage and settled in. I locked the door.

Jeanette couldn't bring herself to go barefoot in the room. She said the carpet was sticky. So she wore her shoes to the edge of the shower stall, then kept her socks on while taking a shower. I'm not sure, but I suspect she also covered the toilet seat with toilet paper.

She wore her shoes back to the side of the bed, finally taking them off and getting in. We immediately rolled together into the middle of the industrial-quality Grand Canyon mattress.

It was late, and we needed to relax, so I put two quarters in the Magic Fingers box at the head of the bed. (It was another bargain. *Triple* the time for just double the regular price.)

Despite my best intentions, the vibrating, V-shaped mattress failed to relax us. And since I had put in *two* quarters, we shook for about forty-five minutes.

When that was finally over, I fell asleep. But Jeanette couldn't get to sleep because of the loud juke box, the roaring trucks and the angry factory workers who were shouting at each other down by the beer joint.

Just then, my wife poked me in the side.

"Somebody is putting a key in the lock on our door," she whispered.

"Don't worry," I mumbled. "Another motel guest is probably just confused about his room number. His key won't fit our lock, and then he'll realize his mistake and leave."

I was wrong. The guy's key *did* work, and he just walked right in. Jeanette screamed. I jumped out of bed, waving my arms like a windmill and trying to think of something intimidating to say. I ended up shouting things like, "Hey, you! Hold it! Wrong room! Back off, Bucko!"

The man muttered something that might have been an apology and left. I locked the door again, but realized that everyone in the motel probably had a key that would unlock our door. Apparently, the Expressway Stay was one of these every-key-fits-every-room places. And here we were, right on the outskirts of Alcatraz Island, Ohio.

Jeanette reminded me that she had *not* been in favor of staying at this particular establishment from the start. And after our encounter with the unexpected visitor, her reluctance was stronger than ever.

"But," I tried to explain, "we've already paid for the room, and by now (well past midnight) we aren't likely to find a room at the Rodeway Inn." So I wedged a chair underneath the doorknob and went back to sleep.

I'm not sure if Jeanette got any sleep that night. But I do know she put her shoes back on. She wanted to be ready to run for it in case another Expressway Stay guest got confused about his room number.

Chapter Eleven

YARD WORK
Planting Tulips in the Sleet

By Nate Adams

*Back in chapter 3, Nate Adams told about asking
Beth to marry him in the middle of a December sleet
storm. Well, the cold, slippery stuff makes a return
appearance here as Nate explains how sleet played a
major role in an unexpected marital adventure.*

I'm no Merlin Olsen, but I like flowers as much as the next
guy. I've never been one to run over poorly placed pe-
rennials with the lawnmower; I don't even go out of my way to
stomp on insects.

But my appreciation of natural beauty doesn't hold a candle
to my wife's. Beth has a love for plants, bushes and flowers that
goes way beyond what might be expected of ordinary human
beings. I view nature as something that serves us. Beth tends
to view nature as something we ought to serve.

So it came as no surprise when, the first autumn after we
moved into our house, Beth wanted to plant tulip bulbs all over
the yard. Initially, the idea appealed to me. I envisioned us with
a shiny new shovel and a bag full of dormant plant life, walking
around our new homestead and carving civilization out of the
wilderness, bulb-hole by bulb-hole.

The concept of "perennial" appealed to me as well. As I
understood it, we'd spend a couple of hours in minimal manual

labor in exchange for years of effortless floral magic. This had to be God's version of the self-cleaning oven, and I was all for it.

Actually, all of this careful tulip selection and bulb-hole digging would have been great if we had planted the bulbs on the same warm, sunny afternoon that we bought them. But for some reason the planting project didn't fit our schedule in September. Or October. Or most of November.

We did talk about it several times, noting that we really did need to get those bulbs in the ground before the weather got too unpleasant. In fact, that's what we were discussing one Saturday in late November as the rain falling outside began to freeze. With pioneer resolve showing all over her face, Beth informed me, "Today is the day. We have to beat the first snow cover!"

Now I don't hate flowers. I don't hate bulb planting. I don't even hate yard work. I just hate freezing in a sleet storm. But my suggestion that we hold off on the bulb burial until next year didn't get much consideration from Beth. She was a woman on a mission.

Once outside, bent over my shovel with buckets of sleet sliding down my neck, I found myself questioning such things as the ethics of throwing some of the bulbs over our shrubs into the neighbor's yard while Beth unsuspectingly planted others. I also questioned whether I might come down with pneumonia and die before these bulbs turned into fine, upstanding tulips.

As it turned out, I survived. And by the time spring came lumbering along, small green shoots had popped up in most of the places we had stuck the bulbs. Little heads of faint color eventually appeared, and we went to bed every night expecting to wake up the following morning to a veritable kaleidoscope of floral color.

In fact, it was one of those very nights that we were lying in bed watching the ten o'clock news. The Chicago weatherman walked out and announced my worst nightmare: "There's a chance of frost tonight in most outlying areas."

We happened to be living in an outlying area, and before the weather report was over Beth was out of bed putting on her jacket. By 10:25 I had joined her in the front yard carrying two old electric blankets, a package of brown paper lunch bags and a flashlight. I was prepared to comply with whatever life-saving methods my wife might ask of me. At her suggestion, I draped the electric blankets over our lilac bushes to guard against frost damage. (At least I convinced her it might be dangerous to actually plug them in. I could picture the cord shorting out in the damp grass and shooting sparks like a Roman candle on the Fourth of July.)

Next, I set to work rescuing the fledgling tulip plants. I dutifully bent over each stalk and covered it with its own paper-bag tent for the night. Actually, I had heard that rabbits love to munch on tulips and couldn't help but feel I was packing thirty-seven upside-down lunches for the neighborhood's woodland creatures. Strange thoughts enter your head when you're forced to leave your warm, dry bed for your cold, wet front yard.

In less than an hour I was back inside, taking off my coat and climbing back into bed. I fell asleep before I finished my grumpy inner debate over the comparative value between a living tulip and a half-dead husband with a severe head cold.

A few weeks later I got over the head cold, and the tulips and lilac bushes had a fine year. But I'm still thinking about hiding this year's garden catalogues.

Chapter Twelve

MACHISMO
The Edge of John's Garage

By Randy Frame

*A former high school football player from the
coal-mining region near Scalp Level, Pennsylvania,
Randy Frame isn't one to turn tail and run from a
good challenge. Especially when he sees it as something that calls into question his masculinity. So it
should come as no surprise that when his friend John
dared him to try something that seemed close to
impossible, Randy accommodated him. What do you
expect from a guy who used to answer to the name
"Earzo"?*

Masculinity. All men possess it. And though we can't
always define it, we can recognize it.

We see masculinity in the man who ends up in another state
before stopping to ask for directions. We see it in the man who
ends up with blisters on his hand before giving in to a tight jar
lid. And of course we see it in the man who, for no apparent
reason, hurls himself headfirst into the sharp corner of a friend's
garage roof.

What? You don't recognize that last example? Well let me
tell you about it. It was Easter Sunday. My wife and I, along with
our infant daughter, had been invited to a friend's home for dinner. The women were indoors putting the finishing touches on
the meal while the men were outside. It was all very masculine.

Some people keep cars in their driveway. My friend John keeps a trampoline. An accomplished gymnast in high school and college, he still showed ample evidence of his old form when occupying the tramp—pot gut notwithstanding.

Up and down. Up and down, up and down, up and. . .

"Oh no," I gasped. He was flying off the tramp. John let out a blood-curdling yell. But before I had time to call an ambulance, he was standing, laughing, on the roof of his garage. In one piece.

I had to admit it looked impressive. *Very masculine,* I thought. *Wonder if I could do it?*

John read my mind. "Why don't you give it a try?" he coaxed. "It's easy."

Sure, I thought. *And it's easy to complete a sixty-yard pass . . . if you're Dan Marino.* Yet I had to admit, this did look "doable." And after all, I'd been on a trampoline before. Once or twice.

The longer I thought about it, the more my competitive instincts began to take over. We're talking about a guy who dislocated a shoulder sliding headfirst into third base in a church softball game. (We lost anyway.) A guy who dislocated a knee executing a fast break in a church basketball game. (I got whistled for traveling.) There was no way I was going to say no to a challenge from an inanimate object, even if it meant risking becoming inanimate myself. Not only would jumping onto John's roof prove me to be a stand-up competitor, but it would also impress my wife, Jeron, like crazy.

But before calling her out to be impressed, I figured it wouldn't hurt to practice the stunt once or twice. Easter Sunday suit and all, I mounted the tramp.

The end of John's garage was about five feet from the edge of the trampoline. He walked me through the strategy, which involved starting at one end of the tramp and working my way toward the garage.

I was loose. I was strategically prepared. (I was terrified.) Off I went, bounding toward the garage, with John looking on, gauging whether I would have the right angle to accomplish this feat. The moment of truth had come. As I hit the tramp for the last time, John sounded the alarm: "Stop!"

But it was too late. Like applying the car brakes after you've already gone over the cliff.

I didn't know exactly what was going to happen to me, but I was fairly certain I wasn't going to enjoy it. I suppose it was something like a skydiver feels after his parachute fails to open.

My nose met the garage first, at about the point where the rain gutter pipe meets the shingled overhang. Down I came, in a heap. My nose was bleeding, but not broken. Vice versa with my glasses. My face bore the scrapes you would expect to see on someone who has just hurled himself into the side of a friend's garage.

Having a bruised and scraped-up face could be a very masculine thing, depending on how it is achieved. Blocking home plate, for example, or falling off a ladder while batting down a hornet's nest. But somehow I didn't feel a strong urge to rush inside to tell my wife what I'd just done, much less get her to come outside and watch me do it again.

Besides, I had lost interest in impressing her. I simply wanted to prove something to myself. Back up on the tramp for a second try. I got to the final jump and waited for John's yell. It didn't come. The next thing I knew, I was standing on top of the garage, both fists raised in victory.

But it was a temporary victory. Soon Jeron came outside, saw my contusions and just shook her head. The fact that I had mastered the trampoline-to-garage-roof leap didn't seem to matter to her. But I had the satisfaction of knowing I had conquered the thing. And I had the nose to prove it!

Chapter Thirteen

CRAZY RELATIVES
Explaining Weird Uncle Otto to My Wife

By Mark MacPhee

Mark MacPhee is the pen name of a writer who has lived in many places, including, for a while, the Orient. But in all his contacts with different people and cultures, he has never met a person quite like his own Uncle Otto. Actually, it never occurred to Mark that his uncle was much different from anybody else's until he introduced Otto to his wife, Sheila. That's when things started getting interesting. This stuff really happened, in fact. Only the names have been changed to protect the parties involved.

I probably should have known something was wrong with Uncle Otto the first time he made us kids eat kohlrabi. I was about ten—my brother, Tim, was nine—and we had just arrived for a weekend visit at Uncle Otto's farm in North Muskola. Otto wasn't really a farmer; he ran his own septic-tank cleaning business. But he and Aunt Rowena lived on about twenty acres just outside of town.

Anyway, about three minutes after my parents dropped Tim and me off, Uncle Otto told us to go out in the garden and pull up a couple of plants that looked like weeds on top but had turniplike globes underneath. He cleaned them off, then pulled out his pocketknife and sliced a wedge for each of us. At the time, it didn't register that he hadn't given either of my cousins a piece. Tim and I were so happy to be "out in the country" that we would have eaten just about anything.

And anything would have been a whole lot better, because two seconds after we bit into the kohlrabi, we were coughing and spitting and wiping our eyes. Can you say hot? That stuff was worse than stepping into a bucket of rubbing alcohol after walking barefoot across a field of thistles.

There stood Otto and my two cousins, hooting and snorting and falling all over each other like they'd just seen a couple of rubes do something really stupid, which is exactly what had happened.

What's really stupid is that Tim and I laughed, too. Despite our burning tongues and watering eyes, we thought Uncle Otto was a comic genius. That impression was confirmed later when Otto pulled the old Whoopee Cushion trick on Tim at the dinner table. Actually, it was that *plus* the snipe hunt and the fake fly-in-the-ice-cube prank that turned us into true believers. As far as we were concerned, every kid ought to have an Uncle Otto.

Trouble is, everybody *doesn't*—or more specifically, my *wife* never had an Uncle Otto, which is probably why she almost left me one August early in our marriage.

It had been one of those sultry nights, and we hadn't slept well. Sheila had gotten up early to get a drink of water. I woke up when I heard her saying, "Mark, there's a strange-looking man sitting on our front porch." Sheila was standing in the bedroom doorway, speaking in a low, measured tone.

"Is he wearing Bermuda shorts and a T-shirt?" I asked.

"Yes," she said.

"Does he have a scruffy old John Deere cap on his head?"

"Yes, and I think he's using snuff."

It was Uncle Otto, of course. Had I been able to view him through my loyal wife's pretty brown eyes, I might have done things differently. Instead, I invited Uncle Otto (and Aunt Rowena, who had been sitting out in the pickup) to break bread—or in this case, toast—with us, which was a mistake.

Otto was so happy to be invited in for breakfast that he said we *had* to let him help with the food. And that, unfortunately, is when Sheila learned the meaning of the word "roadkill." Maybe if I had warned her ahead of time she wouldn't have locked herself in the bathroom when Otto walked back into the kitchen with a fairly stiff squirrel in his hand.

"Oh, Sheila's just a little under the weather," I explained, while Otto parboiled the little fellow he had picked up two towns before ours.

Aunt Rowena and Uncle Otto left later that day, and that night Sheila and I had the first of many long discussions that began something like this:

"I don't want to be rude, Mark. But please don't *ever* let those two inside our house again."

I should have said, "You're absolutely right, dear. That's the last time they'll *ever* cross the threshold of our home!" But I didn't say that, mainly because I had never really thought Uncle Otto was all that odd. I mean, isn't that how uncles are supposed to be?

I've since discovered that my parents and the rest of the MacPhee clan always knew Otto didn't have both oars in the water, but out of kindness they acted as if goofiness were a virtue. If he showed up at a family gathering decked out like Roy Rogers, complete with two *loaded* revolvers dangling at his side, everybody just acted like he'd finished a cattle drive and was "laying over" for a few days. If Otto volunteered to tune up Dad's car, Dad said "Sure," knowing he'd have to take it down to Don's Texaco to get it running right again. Twenty-some years of this can wear out a kid's sense of what's normal and what's not. To us he was just Uncle Otto, a swell guy.

Sheila didn't see it that way.

"I'm serious, Mark, we've got to do something about your uncle," she said after another Uncle Otto visit. We had heard his pickup truck coming down our street, so we hid in the bathroom hoping he would think we were out. But that didn't stop Otto. When we didn't answer the doorbell, he just went around to the back door, came in and got a glass of water. Then he went back outside. We heard the door close behind him, but we didn't hear his truck start up again.

When Sheila and I couldn't stand the suspense any longer, we crept out of the bathroom and peeked through the curtains. There, in the back of his pickup (which was parked in our driveway), Otto was skinning a deer. And the fur, so to speak, was flying.

What else could we do? We came walking out of the house, acting like we hadn't heard the doorbell. Didn't faze Otto; he just cut off a hunk of deer meat and suggested I take it inside and cook it up for supper. (He assured me that the deer was still warm when he picked it up off the side of the road. "When they're warm to the touch and still fairly pliable," he said, "they're safe to eat.")

That's when Sheila and I told him we were just heading out for pizza and asked him and Aunt Rowena to join us. I think that's what they really wanted in the first place, because after a fairly pleasant meal (Sheila played video games the whole time), they said their good-byes and left.

"If he quit bringing dead animals along, would you like him?" I asked Sheila.

"It's not that I don't like him, Mark. It's just that he gives me the creeps. Can't we just tell him never to come here again unless we invite him?"

We decided the next time he and Aunt Rowena showed up, we would have a little talk with them. Give it to them straight. Lay down the law.

Well, we got our chance about three months later when Otto's pickup truck rolled into our driveway.

"Hi Uncle Otto, make yourself at home," I stalled. "We're just heading out for a Cubs game." So much for tough love.

"Really?" His eyes were like a little kid's on Christmas Eve. "I've never been to a professional baseball game."

I felt awful, first because we hadn't really been planning to go to the game, and second because I was about to give the heave-ho to a sixty-seven-year-old man who had never seen the inside of a big-league ballpark. That's when, to my surprise, Sheila went into action.

"You mean you've never been to Wrigley Field?" asked this woman who actually hates baseball. "You'll love it," she said, turning to me. "Let's take them with us!" I guess she figured suffering through a Cubs game would be far better than another at-home Uncle Otto visit.

We got to our seats in the middle of the fifth inning, but that didn't bother Otto or Rowena. Within minutes, both of them were yelling at the left fielder directly below us. Otto bought us hot dogs, and Sheila even ate one of them. For her part, Aunt Rowena had autographs from every usher in our section before the seventh-inning stretch.

On the way home, they talked like a couple of pre-teens leaving a "New Kids on the Block" concert. Then, about three miles from our neighborhood, Otto sat up straight, turned and stared as we passed something on the side of the road.

"You guys ever try 'possum?"

I kept my foot on the accelerator until we came to a restaurant where we could get a meal that had never set foot on asphalt. Rowena and Otto ordered hot dogs. (I guess they had acquired a taste for them at the ballpark.) Sheila resisted the urge to leave the table to go play Pac-Man, and I couldn't remember when the four of us had had such a good time together.

Uncle Otto and Aunt Rowena went back home that night, after telling us how much they had enjoyed themselves. Once the sound of their truck had died in the distance, Sheila admitted to me that she hadn't minded their visit all that much.

All this set me to thinking: If I can just keep Otto from bringing lunch with him when he visits us, I think Sheila might start appreciating his comic genius. Just like my brother and I did the first time we visited him and bit into that raw kohlrabi.

Chapter Fourteen

BURGLARS
Why Men Stalk
Noises in the Night

By Ron R. Lee

As you probably realize from my earlier stories,
I'm sort of a well-intentioned but klutzy husband.
Last time I was checking into a cheap motel; this time
I'm checking out what appears to be a late-night
prowler. What can I say? A husband's gotta do what a
husband's gotta do.

My wife and I have a Nineties kind of marriage. She squashes bugs, and I do laundry. If I'm out of town, she cuts the grass. And when she's out of town, I make sure our preschooler eats enough green vegetables.

We've learned to share and share alike in all our at-home responsibilities. All except one, that is: investigating strange noises in the night. I'm the one who conducts noise investigations, even when it means getting out of a warm bed in the middle of a cold night.

The most recent time it happened, I awoke with a start about two o'clock one morning in the middle of January. I couldn't decide if a noise had awakened me or if it had just been one of those dreams in which you absentmindedly scratch your nose while passing some Hell's Angels on the highway and they come after you with lead pipes.

I decided to ponder the noise vs. dream question awhile before actually getting out of bed. I lay as still as possible, but my adrenalin had my heart doing the bass drum line from a Sousa march. I was pretty sure all was quiet in the house, but I couldn't be certain.

Just then I thought I heard something. And just as quickly, I rationalized that I had only imagined it, deciding not to get out of bed unless I heard it again.

I heard the noise again. It was a scratching sound followed by a muted banging. I tried to convince myself that it was easily explainable. *The wind is blowing a curtain in the family room,* I told myself, *and it's slapping against the nearby floor lamp.* Then I remembered it was January, and all of our windows were closed tight. Or at least they were supposed to be.

If the curtain is blowing, that means somebody is in the house with a stocking cap pulled down over his face. I could picture the guy in my mind, and in the picture, at least, he was climbing through a window. But maybe not. I lay there hoping to get a few more clues to the *exact* location of the noise. I wanted to go directly to that spot when I got ready to investigate. No need to be inefficient at a time like this.

When I heard the sound again, I tried to psych myself up. *What would John Wayne do?* I wondered. *Heck, he'd be the first to say that a* real *man wouldn't be afraid to get beat up while protecting his wife and children.*

Okay, so what would a *normal* person do at a time like this? I thought of some friends, who keep everything from a double-barreled twelve-gauge to a three-foot-long Civil War sword handy for just such occasions. But I'm different. I keep a Louisville Slugger underneath my bed.

I grabbed the baseball bat, held it above my head in what I hoped was a menacing position and crept down the hall, being careful not to awaken my wife.

I figured the intruder was still in the family room, which meant I had the entire length of the house to creep through before I would encounter him. I made it down the first leg of our L-shaped hallway without running into anyone, so I paused at the corner.

What if the burglar is lurking just around this corner? I wondered.

I mustered some manliness and rounded the corner with my Louisville Slugger at the ready. I didn't meet anyone, so I looked into the sewing room just in case he had heard me coming and was trying to hide. But at 2:08 A.M., the sewing room is as dark as Carlsbad Caverns. If the intruder had been in there, I couldn't have seen him unless he had been wearing a stoplight.

I continued creeping down the last part of the hallway. For all I knew, our home invader could be in the bathroom to the left, the entryway to the right or the dining room ahead of me.

With my heart pounding out "Stars and Stripes Forever," I continued my silent creep toward the family room. So far I had noticed no unusual movement, no strange shadows, no weird outlines. But something, probably the cold floor beneath my bare feet, made me shiver. I was still shivering when I reached the door to the family room. My arms were bent in a wind-up, ready to take a Bo Jackson-like swing if the occasion warranted it. But I still didn't see anyone.

I checked the kitchen, the laundry room, the entryway, the bathroom, my daughter's room, the garage. I didn't find anybody. I checked all the windows and doors. All were closed and locked. I checked behind the drapes and in all the closets. Nobody there either.

What could have been making those strange sounds? I checked to see if the furnace or the hot water heater were clinking, popping or wheezing, but I found nothing out of the ordinary. I had to admit that I had gotten out of bed and crept through the house in the middle of the night for nothing.

Just so my excursion wouldn't be a total loss, I got a drink of water. Then I went back to the bedroom and crawled under the covers, putting my Louisville Slugger back underneath the bed.

My feet were cold from sentry duty, and an icy foot is one thing that almost always wakes up my wife. Especially when I scoot it over against her sleeping leg.

"What are you doing?" she mumbled.

"Oh, nothing," I explained. "I just got up to get a drink."

Chapter Fifteen

SWIMSUITS
My Day in Women's Wear

By Harold B. Smith

Family friends had told Harold Smith about Judy Lapham years before he finally met her at the University of Michigan. But when he did make her acquaintance, he knew immediately that she was special. "She laughed at my jokes," Harold recalls. The Smiths have been married more than seventeen years now, and, according to Harold, "She still laughs at my jokes!" A Michigander by birth, Harold has answered to everything from "Wolfman" to "Prune" to "Smitty." In casual conversation, he refers to his wife as "the beautiful Judy."

After seventeen years of marriage, I've learned there are some things about my wife that will never change. For starters, she'll always leave the family car with less than a tenth of a tank of gas left. Further, Judy will *always* need another pair of shoes. "You know, Harold, for the white skirt I borrowed from Debbie."

But even more certain than gas fumes and assorted heels is the assurance that at least once during the year, Judy, a woman with eyes that could make the *Glamour* girl blink with envy, will be on some sort of diet. And with beach weather only months away, Ultra Slim-Fast strawberry has replaced diet Coke as Judy's

81

current beverage of choice.

Actually, Judy hates Ultra Slim-Fast strawberry. It tastes like flavored chalk dust and, if improperly blended, leaves an inch of grit on your back teeth.

But this momentary agony is nothing compared to the true grit Judy says it takes to wear a bathing suit in public. According to Judy, she has enough flaws in her fabric to avoid wearing anything revealing until the year 2051—at which time she'll be around a hundred and, popular wisdom says, much too old for designer swimwear.

For the life of me, I can't figure where my lovely wife learned to equate bathing suits with certain medieval forms of torture. (Of course, she would argue that you could at least hide in an iron maiden.)

I experienced Judy's "body panic" firsthand when we recently went shopping for a new bathing suit.

"Well, hon, what do you think?" my wife-turned-fitting-room-model asked warily.

"I think you look beautiful, sweetie. And I mean it!"

"I don't look like Tubby the Tuba, do I?"

"Of course not," I replied. "Go ahead. Get it."

"You don't think it's too tight, do you?" she said, poking and prodding at her waist, hips, chest, shoulders.

"*No.* You look great. I could eat you up. Go ahead, buy it."

"I need to lose ten pounds."

"You look great!"

"Well, I'll think about it." Translation: "I'm fat."

Back the accursed garment goes, to be replaced by other kinder, gentler, off-the-rack fashions.

Sometime during the evening the desired garment might be purchased, but not without the self-imposed stipulation to lose ten pounds before it's worn or before matching sandals are found—whichever comes last.

Don't get me wrong. I wouldn't want Judy to buy anything that made her look unattractive or feel uncomfortable. It's just that the way she sees herself and the way I see her are two different ways of seeing.

I can't imagine where Judy—or any woman for that matter— learns to be so hard on herself. But on second thought, the pressure points seem obvious: television shows featuring generic perfection; magazine ads with their alluring, airbrushed clones; and men who believe the myth of the perfect body (at least the perfect woman's body).

The rub, of course, is figuring out just what this perfect body looks like. Over the course of history the ideal has ranged from the fleshy, big-hipped madonnas of classical paintings (Judy's favorite period of art) to the muscle maidens of the 1990s. In my own lifetime, Marilyn Monroe gave way to Twiggy, who gave way to Christie Brinkley, who gave way to . . .

Truth be told, the search for the perfect body is over before it begins. In the end, what you're left with is what you started with—the body God gave you. Which is really good news.

Okay. Judy might not think that's the best news she's heard all day, but think of the alternative. She might wind up looking like those women in *Vogue*. Long hair. Long legs. Perfect skin. Perfect teeth.

Perfectly boring.

Boring? Well, how else would you describe someone who looks like everyone else?

But no one looks like Judy. Her eyes? Warm, bright and alive. Her smile? Well, let me put it this way. I've been in classes with Judy where guest lecturers have commented on the supportive and friendly smile of "that woman next to the bald guy."

Am I saying I'd choose my wife over the woman promising me an Aviance night? You bet I would. And it's my privilege to help Judy see herself as she really is—to praise her God-given assets.

That's not to say Judy will ever enjoy shopping for swimwear. But at least she knows she doesn't have to compete with some toothy clone in *Glamour* for my attention. She is free to fine-tune her dieting for health's sake.

Which brings me back to Ultra Slim-Fast strawberry. Four weeks into her latest diet, Judy triumphantly announced at dinner one night that a precious few pounds had been shed. I applauded her willpower. But hearing the announcement, our two sons (ages ten and seven) seemed only mildly impressed.

Said Andrew, our ten-year-old: "You're already the most beautiful mom in the world."

Out of the mouths of babes. Take that, *Glamour* girl.

Chapter Sixteen

CLUTTER
I Am **Not**
Dagwood Bumstead

By Todd Gregory

Todd Gregory is the pen name of a writer and successful businessman who places a high value on productivity and efficiency. His wife, Jennifer, a trained professional in her own right, is more of a free spirit. In some areas, their differences have clear advantages. Todd would readily admit, for example, that Jennifer is a lot more fun at a party. But when it comes to matters such as organizing things around the house, the Gregorys' differences meet head on, in some interesting and surprising ways.

Dagwood, reading the paper on the couch, lifts his feet for Blondie to vacuum underneath them. He lifts them higher and higher, even though Blondie has run off to answer the phone, leaving him with his feet awkwardly pointed at the ceiling. His feet will be in that position for a long time since Blondie is by now having an animated telephone conversation.

For decades, a hundred variations of this gag have amused readers of Blondie and Dagwood and also reinforced a stereotype: Wives are compulsively clean and neat; husbands are oblivious. Husbands scatter socks, shirts, newspapers; wives pick up.

Not true! I happen to be the neatnik in our family, and what's

87

more, I've known a lot more neatnik husbands than wives. But whether the Blondie-Dagwood stereotype is true or not, there *is* one thing you can count on. No matter how a husband or wife approaches household clutter, one spouse will most likely get crosswise with the other.

It all goes back to our childhood. Our parents taught us everything we know about clutter—how to handle it, how to avoid it, how to rationalize it. We don't even suspect that our mates grew up with totally different beliefs about wastebaskets and bulletin boards until the bills and unfiled papers piled high on a desk spill onto the floor. What guilt the messy spouse feels! What righteous anger the neat one summons up— especially if life before marriage was well organized. Who worries in courtship whether the beloved keeps things too neat or too messy? We figure we'll work it out after the wedding. After all, it's just a minor detail.

Some minor detail! You put two people like this together, and you end up with some interesting discussions. I always thought that being neat was a magnificent virtue. But after several years of marriage, I have found that, depending on my attitude, it can be a magnificent pain to my wife, Jennifer.

When I was growing up, simplicity and order were divine doctrines. My mother emphasized simple systems: a place for everything and everything in its place. In keeping with that, she believed in being hospitable but planning hospitality with care. My mother developed a few outstanding recipes and used them over and over, cleaning up the kitchen as she worked. She organized the week into various functions so everything got done in a sensible rhythm. No muss, no fuss.

My wife's parents, on the other hand, were—and still are— spontaneous. They invite guests over at any time, and it took me a few years to figure out that for them—and for Jennifer— guests are the trigger for cleanup. Instead of an ongoing weekly system, clutter is attacked in a great flurry of "hospitality cleanup." People coming means excitement, and straightening and cleaning the house is the prelude to the party. But if no guests are expected, the clutter stays put.

Another difference between us: Jennifer is a registered nurse, so she's a fanatic on cleanliness. No microbe escapes her cleaning rag as she gets down on hands and knees. To her, avoiding clutter is not crucial—but avoiding germs is.

In contrast, I've never gotten trench mouth or strep from household bacteria. But I have often been frustrated by piles of paper, toys and phone books on the kitchen table. Such problems, I declare, could be solved by having a system. And over the years Jennifer has found a sound she truly hates: me uttering the word "system."

It's easy to assume our values brought from childhood are superior. To me, the organized way is the ethical way. To Jennifer, the spontaneous sharing with others and hospitality are more important. Obviously, we need to learn from each other. It's usually a lot more complicated than the need for one spouse to take training from the other—a system, which, as most of us learn, spouses distinctly resist!

All this reminds me of a cartoon strip called "The Born Loser." In the first panel we see a lazy lout in his easy chair, unshaven face and undershirted belly indolently relaxed. His wife confronts him with the accusation, "Just look at you!"

His expression doesn't change, and she says, "Why is it whenever I come into this room, it's disgusting!"

Unperturbed, he looks back at her and delivers the punch line: "You're too hard on yourself, Mother Gargle."

When marriages hit the crunch over cleaning and clutter, interesting things happen. It is our responses that count. When we try to straighten out our mates, we slip on the grease. When we find ways to learn from each other, we clean up our act.

Personally, Jennifer and I need to learn to laugh a little more about clutter and maybe even forget about a microbe or two that might be lurking on the floor. Maybe we can really be creative and get our teenagers organized so *they* clean up the clutter.

Now *that* would be ethically superior!

Chapter Seventeen

HOME REPAIRS
How Many Husbands Does It Take to Fix a Toaster?

By Lyn Cryderman

Call Lyn Cryderman a former newspaper photographer. Call him a world traveler. Call him a ham radio operator. But don't call him a handyman. Because if you did, you'd be lying. Lyn swears he can't fix anything more complicated than a hoagie sandwich. And after reading this story, I believe him.

Three days after our honeymoon it became clear: The success of our marriage depended on my ability to fix the toaster. Not that the broken toaster was an issue—we got three of them as wedding gifts. But when I suggested we toss out the broken one, my wife, Esther, almost dropped her pipe wrench.

"Don't be silly," she said. "Just fix it."

I don't fix toasters. I put slices of bread in them and wait until toast comes out. If, after several minutes, neither toast nor smoke comes out, I grab another toaster out of the closet.

Not Esther. She grew up in a home where men didn't just fix things, they *made* things. Give my father-in-law some scrap metal, a discarded lawn mower engine and a few hand tools, and he'll give you something that works. Heck, it does more than work. You could fly it to New York and back.

93

So you can imagine my bride's reaction more than twenty years ago when I told her I thought the toaster was beyond repair. She got out some tools and fixed it.

Watching Esther in action, I decided it was my husbandly duty to become a fixer. *Becoming a man who would rather sweat a pipe joint than watch Monday Night Football,* I reasoned, *is a small price to pay to enrich my marriage.*

My first step was to join the How-To Book Club. Just for signing up I received four books free: *Home Plumbing Made Easy, Simplified Wiring, Car Maintenance for Beginners,* and of course, *Small Appliance Repair.* I could hardly wait for something to break.

As it turned out, I didn't have to wait long. The battery in our car—a twelve-year-old Volkswagen van—wouldn't charge.

"This shouldn't take long," I told Esther as I nonchalantly grabbed my toolbox and my copy of *Car Maintenance for Beginners.*

Unfortunately, the book didn't explain how to replace the generator on a VW. No problem. I'm a resourceful, think-on-your-feet kind of a guy. A quick survey of the engine compartment indicated that before I could get to the generator I'd have to remove the fan. But to remove the fan, I first had to take the carburetor off the engine. I swallowed hard and began dismantling things. As car parts started piling up on the garage floor, Esther came out to lift my spirits.

"Just think how good you're going to feel when you get it working again," she intoned.

She meant well, but I had heard this motivational gem before, and I knew it to be a lie. Trust me, I *never* feel better after skinning my knuckles, hammering my thumb and self-inflicting a groin injury trying to unfreeze a rusted-on bolt.

My VW repair project required three days of tracking down parts, but I finally located and installed a rebuilt generator, put the fan back where it belonged, bolted the carburetor on and fired her up. To *real* fixers, I suppose, that forty-six-horsepower roar brings tears of joy. The only tears I shed came from my throbbing, swollen thumb. Besides, I've learned to hold off on the customary "successful-repair" celebration.

It's a good thing. The next day brought another dead battery, a service call and a humbling diagnosis from a real mechanic: "Whoever sold you this generator must have taken you for a fool. All you needed was to clean your battery posts." It took three years before my in-laws quit telling the joke about "that time you tried to fix your VW."

That was bad, but things got worse. During a period of temporary insanity, I agreed with Esther that we should move into a house of our own. For three years we stuffed towels around a leaky bathtub. Then one Saturday Esther's dad came for a visit and rebuilt our entire bathroom without once consulting my copy of *Home Plumbing Made Easy.*

For my part, when our washing machine broke down a few weeks later, I grabbed *Small Appliance Repair,* took the thing apart, then called Ernie Poole. Ernie is a skilled technician who has built a profitable business on people like me.

It was after that experience that I made a life-changing decision. I told Esther I had to rescind my earlier naive commitment to become a fixer. Instead, I had to tell her the rotten truth about her husband: He is not a fixer; he will never be a fixer; and it's mostly because he doesn't even want to be a fixer.

Such a smart woman I married. She knew all along I couldn't fix things. "But you always seemed to want to try so I just let you," she explained.

Esther assured me that she still loves me. And when the turntable on our stereo quit turning a month later, she got out my toolbox and fixed it.

Chapter Eighteen

CHRISTMAS TREES
Currier and Ives
Never Met My Wife

By Kevin A. Miller

One of the best things about the Christmas season is all the attendant family traditions that warm the cockles of your heart, right? Well, maybe not. According to Kevin Miller, selecting their first Christmas tree was one of the hardest things he and his wife ever had to do. Kevin is the writer who earlier in this book explained why he looks forward to weekends but shuns clogged toilets. He returns here to tell you how he got burned while shopping for a Christmas tree.

As I write this, it is mid-January, only a few weeks into the endless, barren Chicago winter. I have nothing to look forward to but slush and frozen fingers and huge heating bills and cars that won't start. Yet I am a happy man. The Christmas tree is finally down, and our marriage is safe for eleven more months.

Karen and I got married in the month of September, and the first eighty-four days of our union we lived in unspeakable wedded bliss.

Then came December 7, a day that will live forever in marital infamy. It was a Sunday afternoon, about a week after Thanksgiving, and we were getting holiday fever. The time had come, we decided, to enjoy the time-honored Christmas tradition of every married couple: setting up the Christmas tree.

The very thought sent waves of nostalgia rushing over me. I have seen those Currier and Ives prints: The nineteenth-century husband, mustachioed and rakishly handsome in his top hat, has driven the horse-drawn sleigh out across the back forty to a small stand of blue spruce. His wife, demure and bonneted, sits in the sleigh smiling, a hand-knitted lap warmer across her legs. The husband has ax in hand, and apparently he has felled the nine-foot spruce in a single blow.

For in the next lithograph, the spruce is in the back of the sleigh, and in the final print of the series the tree is standing in the great room of the farmhouse, crisscrossed with cranberry and popcorn strings. The husband and wife are by this time drinking mulled cider by the fireplace.

Then: "Let's go to Sears," my wife suggested.

"Sears?" I asked, my nose wrinkling. "They aren't selling Christmas trees."

"Sure they are," she said. "I saw them in the catalog."

"The catalog? But you don't mean . . ." I could hardly bring myself to say it. "An artificial tree?"

"Sure. What's wrong with that?"

The very question told me something had gone terribly wrong. "Uh, because we don't get artificial trees, that's why. That would be like having a wedding cake made out of cardboard."

"But my family always had an artificial tree," she said, her voice rising a little bit. "They looked great. I don't see anything wrong with them."

Suddenly I realized the woeful inadequacy of our premarital counseling. Our pastor had carefully guided us through discussions of birth control, financial expectations and plans for children. But now, when we hit the real issues, we were left clueless.

For the next half-hour Karen patiently explained to me the merits of an artificial tree. "They don't drop needles," she said.

"You don't have to go out in the cold to get them," she said.

And in a shot where it hurt, she added, "In just a few years, they pay for themselves. Artificial trees actually are much cheaper."

Her case was well-reasoned, sound and tightly argued.

It didn't faze me.

She finally threw up her hands, and we headed out to the back forty to get our wholesome, all-natural, deliciously scented tree. The back forty, however, had been moved to the corner of the K mart parking lot, a tiny patch of asphalt surrounded by a string of bare lightbulbs.

The day, which had started sunny, turned overcast and cold. By the time we reached the lot, it was sleeting. The trees, such as they were, were bundled tight and packed together, about five to the foot. This made it essentially impossible to determine what we were getting. It was like picking out a new car if the dealer had displayed his models by pushing them over a cliff and you picked one from the pile.

Worse, the price was markedly higher than I had imagined. It was, in fact, ten percent above outrageous: almost seven dollars per foot. Even the cheap places charged five dollars per foot, and their trees looked like poster children for a starving-trees charity.

So we drove around to four or five parking lots, corner stands and nurseries until we discovered that: (a) all the lots charge outrageous prices; and (b) our fingers were becoming frost-bitten.

Meanwhile, back at the first lot, we hoped to pick a tree and go when we made another astounding discovery: All the trees were dead or nearly so. Every time we moved one, it shed a pile of brownish-green needles on our feet.

"Where did these trees come from?" I asked the clerk, trying to sound merely curious.

"Nova Scotia," he said.

"Oh."

Then it hit me: To get here all the way from Nova Scotia, this tree must have been cut down on the Fourth of July. While I was at the community park, watching fireworks and eating hot dogs, the citizens of northern Nova Scotia were out cutting down my tree. The result was that the corner of the K mart parking lot now looked like a section from the Petrified National Forest.

But we were here to get a Christmas tree, and get a Christmas tree we would. Karen motioned for me to come over to a tree she had pulled from the rack. "This one looks pretty good," she said hopefully.

"Won't do," I replied. "It's a Scotch pine."

"So?"

"My family always had balsams," I said.

I never knew there were so many disputable issues over a simple tree. But we didn't agree on anything: six-footer vs. eight-footer; long needles vs. short needles; perfect cone shape vs. acceptable bald spot on the back side.

Finally the clerk took pity on us and pulled out what he thought was his best tree. We were tired, so we took it.

At home, Karen started popcorn popping while I set to putting the tree in the stand—an easy job. Then it would be hot chocolate and Christmas lights and tree trimming and romantic music. But after adjusting the tree three times, I couldn't get it straight. On closer examination, I found the tree trunk started out left, bent right and came back left—all in the first eight inches. It must have grown around a rock up there in Nova Scotia.

I had flashbacks to the year my family's neighbor, an engineer in the NASA space program, added water to the tree stand before the tree was fully secured. As the water rose, so did the tree, until it lurched up and over and did a belly flop on their living room floor.

They lost most of their best ornaments, but their marriage survived it, I told myself. *Ours can make it through this.*

And happily, a mere hour later, our tree was standing, nearly vertical and covered with twinkling lights and playful ornaments. Familiar carols were playing on our stereo. Karen and I turned out the room lights and snuggled on the sofa.

"Isn't this romantic?" Karen said, in a hushed voice.

"It sure is," I agreed. "After all that struggle, it's worth it. Our tree is beautiful."

We sat entranced and silent. The only sounds we could hear were the beautiful strains of "Away in a Manger"—and occasionally, a dead pine needle dropping to the floor.

Chapter Nineteen

DATE NIGHT
Dinner and a Movie

By Tim Stafford

*Ask Tim Stafford what first attracted him to his
wife, Popie, and he'll tell you, "She laughed at a
stupid commercial on TV." Ask him who his favorite
comedian is, and he'll say, "Silas, my four-year-old."
Clearly, this is a family that knows how to have a
good time. Tim and Popie live in Santa Rosa, California, with their preschool comedian, Silas, and his
siblings, Katie and Chase.*

Five months ago we celebrated our tenth anniversary,
spending four days at a Victorian bed and breakfast on
the wild Mendocino coast. Those four days felt like a huge sigh
of relief. We read, slept, walked, talked and regained our bal-
ance.

But tonight it feels like we haven't seen each other since.
Popie's been taking night and weekend classes; I've been fac-
ing deadlines. We've been preoccupied. We haven't had time
for a date like the one we're having tonight. Unthinkable lux-
ury: dinner and a movie.

The babysitter is late. (But who would complain? Baby-
sitters are like gold.) Worse, *Popie* is running late. I try not to
worry about it.

"We need to go in about fifteen minutes," I warn gravely.

103

Then, "We really ought to be going now." Finally, urgently, "We need to go." I end up in the car, motor running, watching the front door, resisting the temptation to honk.

After ten years we find ourselves falling into these stereotypes. I hate to be late. She hates to be early. Ten years ago it might have prompted an attempt to settle our differences. Now we don't have time to worry about such petty matters. We live with them. We have accepted our differences, though not always gladly.

She appears, looking beautiful. I glance at my watch and see we will be on time. I find myself slightly nervous, an echo of how I would have felt years ago when we were courting. When you don't go out for a long time, you lose the rhythm of it. I want it to be a good time. I want Popie to like being with me. But in the car we don't have too much to say. As we were leaving, our six-year-old, Katie, burst uncharacteristically into tears. Popie is thinking about that.

I need to run over to the money machine on the corner, so after parking I send Popie ahead in case there's a line for the movie. Naturally, there are three people ahead of me at the money machine. I grab the cash that pops out of the little door and jog to the theater. By the time I reach Popie she's been to the head of the line once and has started over again.

But in no time we're inside. We buy a small popcorn and a box of Junior Mints, a combination that reminds me of childhood trips to the movies. And there's still plenty of time and plenty of seats. Someday I will have to stop worrying about being late. We dive into the popcorn. "Butter flavor" is soon all over our hands. We always finish the popcorn before the credits are done; tonight is no exception.

"Aren't you glad we're both pigs?" I ask. "It would be terrible to be married to someone who found this distasteful."

"Save some of the mints for the kids," she says. How is it

she always thinks of them?

The lights dim, and the movie begins.

"Oh, nice," I murmur as the title dissolves into shimmering moonbeams.

"The credits," I explain, glancing at her.

Not everybody would appreciate what I appreciate in a movie. When Dean Martin's velvet voice pours out "That's Amore," I suspect I am going to like this film. Somebody made it with a sense of humor. I look over at Popie to see whether she likes it too. Our eyes meet. She is smiling with pleasure. What a joy to be married to someone who likes the same movies you do. Soon it is over, and we shuffle patiently toward the door.

Outside the air is frosty, and I wrap my arm around her waist. I am gaining confidence. This could be a good night. The Restaurant Matisse is two streets over and a block to the left, and we walk, chatting about the bookstore we pass, then the paint store.

Then we leave the cold and go into the bustling, cheery (expensive) restaurant. There are two tiny flowers by our cutlery. Popie puts them into her pocket for Katie. We order. The food comes, and we begin to eat, exclaiming at the luscious scallops, the dark, pungent sauce. And like two weary people sinking into the sofa at the end of the day, we plunge into conversation. I stop thinking about what to say or how we are doing or whether this will be a good night. I am just opening up my life and letting it pour out, as is she. The waitress comes and goes, but we seem enclosed in a small bright globe. We linger. Do we want dessert? We ponder the menu and decide we will not.

Out in the cold we continue talking, as though we might go on forever, talking while we amble on over the hills and into the sea, not noticing until the waves covered our heads. We get in the car and go home. It is not too late. We pay the babysitter, light some candles and put on soft music. And do what they say comes naturally.

I know not all marriages are like ours. Tonight, at a table near ours, Popie pointed out a quiet battle in progress, tears and all. But our hardness, when it comes, is more often like the hardness of winter, when the sun comes up late and goes down early and you settle into a numbed, close-the-door-it's-freezing-out-there routine. It's not horrible by any means. But compared to our summery times, it's not terribly happy either.

That's why we need, much more often than we take it, a night like tonight. Dinner and a movie. Such a simple thing, yet it reminds us of who we are and why we are married. I think of something Popie says about God: how you can worry that your relationship with Him has gone cold, that you've lost your spiritual edge. You can think it will take a lot of time, a month or so of spiritual discipline, to get going again with Him.

Then you sit down and discover, in just minutes, that you don't have to do a thing—except take some time. Be alone with Him. In what feels like no time you are caught up again in your love.

Index